Why Should We Recycle?

by Mrs. Houchin's class
with Tony Stead

capstone®
classroom

Mrs. Houchin's second grade class has been talking about why we think recycling is important. Here are a few reasons why we think people should recycle.

Recycling paper means that we save animal habitats.

Recycling can also keep people and animals safe from sharp objects.

Another reason why we should recycle paper is so landfills do not get overfilled.

This means that there will be fewer landfills to pollute our Earth!

Recycling metal means that we can build more homes and cars. Metal is the most recycled material in the world! This means that there will be more homes for people to live in and sharp objects will not hurt you.

We also should recycle metal because it can save energy.

This means that an amazing amount of energy is saved in the steel factory because they are working with recycled metal and creating new metal. The energy saved is enough to power 18 million homes.

Recycling glass saves enough electricity to light a 100-watt light bulb. This means less energy will be wasted.

We also should recycle because it can keep our environment clean and safe. This means that animal homes will not be cut down and there will be more wildlife.

Here are some things that you can recycle to keep our world cleaner and safer. If everyone recycled our world would be a better and cleaner place to live. What do you think is the most important reason to recycle?